101 Tax Investigation Secrets Revealed

By

James Bailey

Publisher Details

This guide is published by Tax Insider Ltd, 3 Sanderson Close, Great Sankey, Warrington WA5 3LN.

'101 Tax Investigation Secrets Revealed' first published in June 2013, second edition May 2015.

Contents

Contents

Chapter 4. Penalties For Lost Tax

Chapter 5. Disclosure

Chapter 6. Tax Avoidance, Tax Evasion, And Tax Fraud

Contents

Chapter 11. Conclusions

About This Guide

There are numerous types of tax investigation, and this book summarises them all, and explains what is involved.

We shall also be looking at the legal background to HM Revenue & Customs' powers to enquire into your tax affairs, and at the consequences of being found to have got something wrong.

Finally, we will consider ways to protect yourself, both from being investigated in the first place, and how to minimise the damage if you are unfortunate enough to be the subject of an enquiry by HM Revenue & Customs (HMRC).

Chapter 1.
The Basics

1.   What Is A Tax Investigation?

A tax investigation is triggered when HMRC uses its statutory powers to look at your tax return and/or the accounts for your business in order to satisfy themselves that they are correct.

Most tax returns and business accounts that are sent to HMRC are simply filed into the system so that the amounts of tax that you owe can be calculated and the Statements of Account can be sent out. Most tax returns are never actually looked at or checked for accuracy.

However, a small percentage of these tax returns will be investigated further by HMRC.

A tax investigation by a local tax office can take several forms, explained in Tips 2 to 6.

2.   Compliance Check

Compliance checks are becoming a more important part of HMRC's enforcement policy. They involve visiting a business (which HMRC have the legal power to do, if necessary without your consent) to make sure that proper books and records are being kept, or that PAYE is being operated properly on the wages paid to employees.

Other examples are checks on VAT or in the case of the building trade, the Construction Industry Scheme.

3.   Aspect Enquiry

The commonest type of enquiry is an 'aspect enquiry', where the inspector simply asks one or two questions to satisfy himself or herself that a particular point in the tax return is correct; a common example is a check that a capital gain in your tax return has been correctly calculated.

These are not usually particularly serious and are usually dealt with in a matter of weeks. However, in some cases they can be very time-consuming, particularly when complex legal points are involved and, very occasionally, they can expand into a 'full enquiry'.

4.   Full Enquiry

A full enquiry is when HMRC goes right through your tax return to make sure that the personal information and business accounts that you have filed are correct. This can be a very thorough and stressful process. Full enquiries used to be the main type of work done by tax inspectors, but these days they are less common, with aspect enquiries representing the majority of HMRC enquiries.

5.   Other Types Of Enquiry

Any type of tax return may be the subject of an enquiry by HMRC, so a return of inheritance tax filed on the occasion of someone's death could be the subject of an enquiry. Where the major inheritance tax reliefs are being claimed (such as business property relief or agricultural property relief), or where valuations of property are involved, inheritance tax enquiries are becoming increasingly common.

Stamp Duty Land Tax (SDLT) is another tax that is now more subject to enquiries than in the past, probably due to the increasing number of SDLT avoidance schemes that are being marketed.

It should not be forgotten that HMRC are responsible for policing the National Minimum Wage Legislation, and they also conduct enquiries to see that this legislation is being complied with.

6.   The COP 9 Enquiry

The final type of enquiry is known in the trade as a 'COP 9' enquiry – short for Code of Practice 9, which is a document issued to a person whom HMRC suspect has been committing tax fraud.

The Contractual Disclosure Facility (CDF) is effectively an offer from HMRC saying that 'we know you have committed fraud, but if you confess to it and give us the full details we will not prosecute you. Instead we will just take the tax, interest on the tax, and financial penalties from you'.

If you get a letter from HMRC that includes a CDF form and the leaflet COP 9 – 'Code of Practice 9' – then the situation is very serious and you absolutely must get professional advice.

I have known people to take the alternative course, which is to flee the country, but I obviously cannot recommend this!

A CDF/COP 9 letter means that HMRC consider that they can probably prove that you have committed tax fraud.

Most of what is said in this book about conventional local investigations does not apply to a CDF/COP 9 enquiry. It really is a completely different matter, and let's hope you never get one. If you do, then you should go straight to a specialist in tax investigations – or if you already have an accountant, ask him or her to recommend a specialist in tax investigations. Accountants in general practice will (or should) agree that they simply do not have either the time or the expertise to deal with a CDF/COP 9 enquiry.

7.   Why Are Tax Enquiries Started?

In short, the inspector starts investigations because he or she can! HMRC has power under the tax legislation to inquire into any tax return.

They do not have to have a reason and in fact they actually do look at quite a number of tax returns every year on a purely random basis.

A 'tax investigation' can thus be similar to a lottery – if your number comes up they will open an enquiry on you.

Other investigations are started because HMRC has specific information about your business. They may have received information from an informer, or they may have picked something up while investigating someone else's tax affairs.

An investigation can also be triggered if they are aware of any particular risks in your business. A good example might be a pub, which is primarily a cash business so it is comparatively easy to conceal some of the takings.

HMRC also has software that interrogates their databases and the figures that have been submitted.

The software can identify anomalies where, for example, the relationship between the purchases and the sales appears to be out of kilter with the relationship that you'd expect for that particular kind of business.

However, more often they will have some reason to suspect that there is something wrong and rather than the return being investigated at random they will have actually flagged it up as one that they are going to investigate. Essentially they look for certain triggers.

I have already mentioned that HMRC's software will spot anomalies in accounts – such as where the purchases and sales are not what you would expect for that sort of business.

HMRC are very fond of what they refer to as **gross profit rates (GPR)**. The GPR of a business is the percentage of profit made from the purchases and sales, before taking into account the overheads such as staff costs, rent, advertising and so on (which vary much more from business to business). They have access to extensive statistics about the likely GPRs for various types of business in their local area and nationally, and are likely to investigate accounts which show different figures.

They also look for unexpected evidence of wealth. For example if you declare income which seems just enough to support you and your family and suddenly you start declaring an amount of interest from a bank account that suggests a substantial deposit in that bank account, then they might investigate to find out where you got the cash to open the bank account.

Of course there might be a perfectly genuine reason such as an inheritance but HMRC might well investigate your return to find out where the money came from.

Also, I am afraid that quite often investigations are opened as a result of informers. When I worked as a tax inspector we used to get a lot of informers and I am sure that this is still the case.

I suppose the most likely informers are disgruntled employees. We used to get a number of people who had left or been sacked or had had a disagreement with their employer, who got their own back by telling us about tax irregularities they knew or suspected were going on.

Next are spouses and girlfriends or boyfriends.

I think I can say that anyone fiddling their taxes should make sure they are good to their employees and don't fall out with their husband or their wife because they really are one of the most common sources of information!

On one occasion my informer was someone who was negotiating to buy a business and the proprietor of the business had been stupid enough to show him two sets of books – one he used for HMRC and the other one he claimed to be the real set, showing a much higher profit. The purchaser came straight round to the tax office and told me about it.

The above instances highlight the fact that HMRC do not carry out all their investigations at random by any means. In many cases they either have specific information about tax irregularities, or the accounts look strange compared to others for similar businesses.

To summarise, there can be three key reasons for an investigation:

1. You are randomly selected.
2. HMRC has specific information on your business (e.g. via an informer).
3. Your accounts look odd compared to the accounts of other similar businesses.

There is no particular bias towards newer or older businesses, though it might well be the case that a newly started business that is particularly unusual could be selected for an investigation, almost as a fact-finding exercise.

Chapter 2.
The Meaning Of Words

8.   Key Words In Tax Investigations

Before we start looking at different types of investigation, the powers of HMRC, and the penalties for incorrect returns, there are certain words with specialised meanings that we need to understand.

These are 'reasonable' (Tip 9), 'deliberate' (Tip 10), and 'deliberate with concealment' (Tip 10).

9.   What Is 'Reasonable'?

'Reasonable' is one of those words that means different things to different people – everyone thinks that he or she is a reasonable person, and we have all appealed to another person to 'be reasonable'. In tax, as we shall see, there are several types of 'reasonable'.

If you take 'reasonable care' when preparing and submitting your tax returns then, even if they are incorrect, you are not liable to a penalty. What constitutes 'reasonable care' depends partly on your own level of knowledge about tax, but if you do not understand something HMRC expect you to take advice. If you do use the services of a tax adviser you are not off the hook, however. You are also expected to take 'reasonable care' in choosing an appropriately qualified adviser, and to check what he or she has produced.

Two true stories illustrate the distinction:

In the first case, there was a technical mistake in calculating the capital gains tax due in an elderly businessman's tax return. The mistake involved highly complex tax law – indeed, when I was called in to advise, I was able to find an example of a tax inspector making exactly the same technical error in another case. The tax return had been prepared by a reputable firm of chartered accountants, and had then been checked by the businessman's own in-house accountant, who told the businessman the return was correct. On this basis he signed the return without checking it personally. Despite the fact that he would almost certainly not have spotted the error, HMRC took the view that because he had not personally attempted to check the return, he had not shown 'reasonable care', and they charged a (small) penalty.

The second case is one that came before the tax tribunal in 2012. The taxpayer's return, prepared by his accountants, included a claim for relief from capital gains tax to which he was not entitled. He had read an article that made him think he could make the claim, and had sent a copy to his accountants, who had in turn consulted a specialist, who (wrongly) said the claim was valid. The Tribunal took the view that the taxpayer had taken 'reasonable care', even though those he had relied on had made a mistake about the relief claimed, and so no penalty was due.

'Reasonable' also crops up in the case of 'reasonable excuse'. If you are late in either making a return required by law, or in paying tax that is due, then in order to avoid a penalty, you will have to show that you had a 'reasonable excuse' for the delay. Not surprisingly, HMRC have a very narrow view of what is and is not a 'reasonable excuse'. They will for example accept serious illness or the death of a close relative, or a fire or flood destroying the relevant papers, but with very few exceptions they will not accept shortage of funds or reliance on another person (for example, going on holiday and asking someone else to post the return or the cheque).

Finally, but most importantly, when we examine the powers that HMRC have to investigate and gather facts, we will find that HMRC themselves have to meet the 'reasonableness' test. For example, all the powers to gather information from the taxpayer and from third parties are subject to the proviso that the information requested must be 'reasonably required' for the purposes of the tax enquiry. This can be extremely important, as we shall see.

10. 'Deliberate' And 'Deliberate With Concealment'

If a return is incorrect in any way, then the level of penalty due will depend on whether or not the inaccuracy was 'deliberate'.

It is easiest to understand the difference between a 'deliberate' mistake and a 'careless' mistake by looking at a few examples. The following are taken from HMRC's own 'Compliance Handbook':

Example of careless inaccuracy

> Paul, a self-employed plumber, does not pay much attention to his record-keeping responsibilities and has no structured system for making sure that his records are accurate.

> When Paul completes his SA tax return he cannot be certain that his figures are correct and is unable to check them. This attitude towards record-keeping indicates a lack of reasonable care.

Example of deliberate inaccuracy

> Sarah takes £50 per week from her takings as 'pocket money'. This money goes unrecorded when she adds up her weekly takings and enters the total into her records. Those records form the basis of Sarah's turnover figure on her tax return, which she knows to be incorrect.

> Sarah has deliberately recorded the wrong figure of sales in the business records. However there is no evidence of additional artificial or false records being produced to conceal this deliberate inaccuracy.

A deliberate inaccuracy is more serious if it also involves 'concealment'. Again, this is best explained by an example from the HMRC manual:

Example of deliberate inaccuracy with concealment

> Mary is a self-employed hairdresser. During a compliance check of her Self Assessment return, you discover interest from a bank account that she has not declared in her return. Mary produces a letter from her aunt to support her explanation that the source of the funds in the bank account was a gift from her aunt.
>
> During the compliance check you establish that Mary had not received any money from her aunt, the money was undeclared income from the business. She had taken active steps to conceal the inaccuracy by creating an alternative explanation for the source of the funds in her undeclared account.

As we shall see, these words, 'reasonable', 'careless', 'deliberate' and 'concealment' are of great importance in how a tax enquiry is conducted, and particularly so when it comes to working out any penalties that may be imposed for mistakes in tax returns.

Chapter 3.
HMRC Powers

11.   Information Notices

HMRC have considerable powers to require information from people about their own and other people's tax returns.

Information notices

There are four types of information notice:

- Taxpayer notice – this is a notice to a taxpayer requiring them to provide such information as is 'reasonably required' to check their tax position.
- Third-party notice – this is a notice to a third party to provide information about someone else's tax. The obvious example would be a notice to a bank to produce information about accounts held by the person under enquiry.
- Identity unknown and identification notices – these two types of notice are very unusual and it is probably safe to say that you will not come across them – they are mainly used in the course of major investigation projects.

An information notice must specify the information required, and that information must be in the 'possession or power' of that person – in other words it must be information they have actually got (such as copies of sales invoices) or which they can reasonably be asked to produce (such as an analysis of the claim for 'repairs' in a set of accounts).

Certain information cannot be the subject of an information notice:

- Documents over six years old (with a very few exceptions).

- Documents prepared for the purposes of an appeal concerning tax.
- 'Personal records' – these are records concerning a person's physical, mental or spiritual welfare, so for example your desk diary is not excluded but your medical records are.
- Journalistic material – that is, information a journalist has acquired for the purpose of writing an article.
- Legally privileged material – books have been written about precisely what this means, but broadly speaking, it means communications between lawyers (not accountants or tax advisers) and their clients.
- Auditors' statutory audit papers – this only applies to papers concerned with the statutory audit under the Companies Act or similar legislation – it does not apply to ordinary accounts preparation documents.
- Tax advisers' papers giving tax advice – note this only applies to the adviser, who cannot be asked to disclose the advice he or she gave you – it does not apply to you, the client, who can be asked what advice you were given.

A tax inspector can give an information notice on his or her own responsibility in many cases, but in certain cases needs the formal approval of the Tax Tribunal.

12. The Tax Tribunal And Appeals

Approval for certain information notices must be given by the Tax Tribunal, which is an independent judicial body that not only gives its approval to the exercise of certain HMRC powers, but also deals with disputes between HMRC and taxpayers, as we shall see later (Chapter 9).

It is unusual for the Tribunal's approval to be needed for a notice to a taxpayer, but it is necessary for a third-party notice unless the taxpayer has given his or her consent to the issuing of the notice. It is almost always necessary in the case of the other two more esoteric notices (identity unknown and identification) but these need not concern us here.

In general, the taxpayer is not informed of the request to the Tribunal for approval of a notice, and has no right to be heard by the Tribunal before they approve the notice.

A taxpayer can appeal against a notice issued by an inspector (but not one approved by the Tribunal), but the grounds of appeal are very limited.

The appeal can either be on the grounds that the information in the notice is not 'reasonably required' to check the tax position, that the information called for is on the list of information set out in Tip 11 which cannot be asked for, or that (in the case of a third-party notice) it would be 'unduly onerous' to provide the information required.

A taxpayer cannot appeal against a notice which has been approved by the Tribunal (except by seeking a Judicial Review, which is a hideously complex and expensive process), and nor can a taxpayer appeal against a notice to produce any 'statutory records'.

'Statutory records' means records required to be kept for the purposes of complying with the tax legislation, so they would include sales and purchase records, invoices, bank statements, VAT invoices, and so on.

A common area of dispute on the question of what records are 'reasonably required' is the matter of private bank statements. If HMRC are investigating the tax affairs of a company, they will frequently ask for copies of the directors' personal bank statements covering the period (usually a year) under enquiry. Are these 'reasonably required'? If (as commonly happens) the directors have used their personal bank accounts or credit cards to pay company expenses, then it is difficult to resist the request for at least the statements covering the transactions concerned. Nevertheless, any such request should be considered carefully before either complying or objecting on the grounds they are not 'reasonably required' – but remember, if the Tribunal gave its approval to the information request, you are wasting your time, because there is no appeal possible against the request.

13.   Penalties For Failing To Produce Information

Normally, HMRC will begin by simply asking for the information, and giving a 'reasonable' amount of time to produce it – typically between 30 and 60 days, depending on the complexity of the information required.

If the information is not produced, the next step is the issue of a formal information notice like those described in Tips 11 and 12.

This notice will itself give time to produce the information. There is no minimum or maximum time required, but typically, given the notice comes after a previous request for the information, the time given will be 30 days.

The penalty for failing to comply with an information notice within the time specified is £300, with a further £60 **per day** until the information is supplied.

All of which means that if you receive a request for information, and you think it is not 'reasonably required' by the inspector, then you should not ignore it!

14. HMRC Visits And Inspections

As well as requiring taxpayers to provide them with information, HMRC have powers to visit and 'inspect' business premises.

It is important to be clear about the extent of these powers, because there is no point in resisting in a case where HMRC are within their rights, but equally, you should not let them overstep those powers.

Subject always to the 'reasonably required' test that also applies to information notices, HMRC may visit 'business premises' and 'inspect' both 'business assets' and 'business documents'.

'Business premises' means premises from which a business is carried on. If the business is run from the taxpayer's home, then HMRC may visit the parts of the house used for the business, but not the private areas. To use HMRC's own example:

Example of a business run from home

> Horace runs a Bed & Breakfast business from his home. You are allowed to inspect empty guestrooms and any other public areas set aside for guests. You are not allowed to enter or inspect any of the bedrooms or other rooms used solely by Horace and his family.

'Business assets' means items used in the business such as machinery and plant, computers, storage facilities, and so on.

'Business documents' means the 'statutory records' of the business – as described in Tip 12 for the purpose of information notices, and are subject to the same restrictions – legal privilege, personal records, etc. (see Tip 11).

The meaning of 'inspect' is the most important definition here. If, like me, you are a fan of courtroom dramas and police procedurals, you will have some idea of the way these things are done in the USA, and the system in the UK is similar.

It has been said that, 'Inspect is by eye and search is by hand', which gives a good rule of thumb for the distinction, but a few examples (again, genuine ones from HMRC's own internal instructions) will make the limits of 'inspect' clearer:

Example of what is and is not meant by 'inspect'

1. *You are walking along a corridor with a representative of the business and come to a door in the corridor. He goes through but the door slips and closes in front of you. You may touch the door to open it and continue.*

2. *You are shown into a room in which the books, records and invoices you asked for have been placed on a table for your inspection. You are allowed to open the files and boxes of records that have been collected. You are allowed to walk around and look at the pictures on the wall. You are not allowed to open the filing cabinet in the corner just to see what is in it.*

3. *You are shown into a room in which the accounting records you asked for have been placed on a table for your inspection. You are told the invoices are in the filing cabinet in the corner. You may open the filing cabinet to inspect any invoices that you may want to.*

4. *You are inspecting premises used in connection with taxable supplies and there is a delivery van in the yard waiting to offload goods. You are allowed to open the door – remember health and safety – as means of transport such as cars and vans are, for these purposes, premises. You may look at the boxes inside. You are also allowed to climb*

inside and look at the boxes you cannot see from outside. You should ask the trader to open any box you want opening so you can check the tax position of what is inside. It should be very rare to want to inspect goods waiting to be sent out for delivery. You are not allowed to open the driver's holdall.

Except in exceptional circumstances, HMRC are required to give at least seven days' notice of a visit.

You have a right to refuse the HMRC officers entry, but be careful. The consequences will depend on whether the visit has been authorised by the Tax Tribunal or not. Normally, the decision to arrange the visit will have been arrived at internally and the Tribunal will not have been involved, but in more serious cases, and nearly always in the case of unannounced visits, formal authority will have been obtained from the Tribunal. If you refuse or obstruct the visit in these circumstances, then there is an initial penalty of £300, followed by daily penalties of up to £60 until you allow the visit.

In general, provided you are given reasonable (at least seven days') notice, it is unwise to be obstructive about it – but make sure you have your tax adviser there – more (much more!) about this later.

15. Enquiries Into Tax Returns – Time Limits

You may have heard talk about the 'enquiry window', meaning the time limit for HMRC to begin their enquiries into a tax return. The length of this 'window' varies – for example, the 'window' for a return of Stamp Duty Land Tax is nine months after the return is filed, but the commonest 'window' you will come across is that for self assessment returns (income tax, capital gains tax, and corporation tax), and this window is 12 months from the date the return is filed.

For example, the income tax and capital gains tax self assessment for the tax year 2013/14 was due to be filed by 31 January 2015. If it was in fact filed on that day, then HMRC have until 31 January 2016 to open an 'enquiry' into that return. If, however, the return was filed earlier, say on 1 July 2014, then HMRC's 'enquiry window' will have closed on 1 July 2015.

Once the enquiry window has closed, however, HMRC can still open an enquiry into the return if they can show they have made a 'discovery'.

16.   What Is A 'Discovery'?

Because only by making a 'discovery' can HMRC start enquiring into returns after the enquiry window has closed, the question of what constitutes a 'discovery' is hotly disputed between tax advisers and HMRC, and there have been many court cases on the subject.

This is a very complex area of law, but broadly speaking, in order to 'discover' that tax has or may have been underpaid, the inspector has to show that the information in the return itself was not sufficient for him or her to have been able to see the possible problem.

When A Discovery Is Possible

John sells a house (not his main residence) during the tax year 2014/15. He owned the house before 31 March 1982, so the CGT rules require him to use its market value on that date as the 'cost' for the purposes of working out the amount of his capital gain. He knows the house cost £30,000 when he bought it in 1979, so he guesses at a March 1982 value of £50,000, and ticks the box on his return to say that the return includes estimated figures.

Jill sells the house next door, and like John, she owned it before March 1982. Jill pays a chartered surveyor for a professional valuation as at March 1982, and in her return she uses the 'white space' to include this note: 'March 1982 value of Sunny Cottage at £40,000 provided by Mr Jones FRICS, of Smith and Smith, Chartered Surveyors, in a formal valuation dated 15 August 2015'.

John has not done enough to ensure that after the first anniversary of filing his 2014/15 return it cannot be the subject of an enquiry. He has not specified which value is the subject of an estimate (though it is pretty obvious that it is the 1982 value), and he has not made it clear that the estimate is his rough and ready one rather than one by a competent professional.

HMRC might argue the point but in my view Jill has. The belt and braces approach would have been to actually enclose a copy of the valuer's report with the return, but that would require the return to be filed on paper rather than online, as the facility to attach PDFs to online returns would probably not cope with a document the size of a 'red book' valuation.

17.   Time Limits For Amending Returns

It should be remembered that similar time limits apply for the taxpayer to amend his or her return if the taxpayer realises that he or she has made a mistake. For personal and company tax returns, this time limit is the first anniversary of the date for filing the original return. Within this time period, it is possible to amend anything in the return without HMRC being able to say that the original return was incorrect – though if the amendment results in more tax being due, they can and will charge interest on it from the date it should have been paid.

Amending A Return

John happens to get talking to Jill about the house sales in the previous example. He is worried that he may have overestimated the March 1982 value. The filing date for his 2014/15 return is 31 January 2016, so he has until 31 January 2017 to amend his return. He does so on 31 July 2016, within the time limit, changing the March 1982 value to £40,000, the same as used by Jill. This change results in additional CGT payable of £2,800, and he will have to pay interest of £42 (£2,800 at 3% p.a. for six months), but there will be no penalty for an incorrect return.

Amending his return like this means that HMRC's enquiry window restarts, and does not close again until 30 September 2017 (being the 'quarter day' following the first anniversary of the date of the amendment). Notice, however, that because he has not included any more information about the way he arrived at the valuation, in practice HMRC can still make a 'discovery' after that date.

Note that the time limits for amendments by the taxpayer are more generous than those for HMRC – whereas HMRC have until the first anniversary of the date the return was actually filed (if it was filed within the time limit), the taxpayer has until the anniversary of the statutory filing date, even if in fact he or she filed the return before then. This is of course a deliberate policy, to encourage early filing by taxpayers.

Once HMRC have begun an enquiry into a tax return, it is too late to amend it, though HMRC can themselves amend it if agreement cannot be reached – this is known as a 'jeopardy amendment' and can be appealed against in much the same way as a tax assessment.

18.   Normal Time Limits For Assessing Tax

There are numerous time limits governing how long after the end of a tax year (or a company's period of account, or the end of a VAT quarter, etc.) HMRC can take steps to recover any underpaid tax – known as assessing time limits.

These time limits depend on the reason for the tax being due.

Bear in mind that all these time limits only come into effect if HMRC have made a 'discovery' as described previously (Tip 16). In the absence of a 'discovery' the time limit remains the first anniversary of the filing of the return.

The 'normal' time limit is four years from the end of the relevant period, and this one works both ways – it is the time limit for HMRC to claim tax for an earlier year, and it is also the time limit for the taxpayer to make a claim if he or she realises that he or she has paid too much tax.

Note – the time limit for a taxpayer to make an 'overpayment' claim is four years, but be careful – if the overpayment relates to a claim that is normally made in a tax return, then the shorter time limit for amending the return may apply – this is outside the scope of the present book.

If HMRC can show that the tax is unpaid because of the taxpayer failing to take 'reasonable care', then the time limit is extended to six years from the end of the period in question.

Normal Time Limit And Six-Year Time Limit

The self assessment return for the tax year 2009/10 had to be filed by 31 January 2011. Assuming the return was actually filed on that day HMRC have until 31 January 2012 to enquire into the return.

If, however, they can show they have made a 'discovery' that tax has not been paid, they have until 5 April 2014 (four years after the end of the 2009/10 tax year) to make an assessment to collect the tax.

If they can show that the tax is unpaid because the taxpayer did not take 'reasonable care' with his or her 2009/10 return, however, they have until 5 April 2016 to make an assessment.

19.   The 20-Year Time Limit

In certain circumstances, HMRC can go back as far as 20 years. These are:

- Where tax has been lost because of the 'deliberate' actions of the taxpayer – we have seen what 'deliberate' means for this purpose (Tip 10).
- Where the tax was lost because the taxpayer failed to notify HMRC that they should complete a tax return (for years before the rules changed in 2008/09 this gets a bit more complicated and involves showing 'negligence' by the taxpayer – not worth exploring here).
- The tax lost involves a notifiable tax avoidance scheme, and the scheme was not notified to HMRC – more on this in Chapter 6.
- The tax is VAT and involves certain specific types of avoidance of VAT.

Under no circumstances can HMRC go back beyond 20 years.

20.   Death And Taxes

In the case of a person who has died, the time limits are considerably shorter, so that the executors can wind up the estate without worrying about unexpected tax bills.

The normal time limits apply to the executors for any tax due from the estate on income or gains arising during the period after death, but for periods before the person died:

- any assessment must be made within four years of the end of the year of assessment in which they died, and
- for income tax and capital gains tax that assessment can only cover tax for a year of assessment that ended less than six years before the date of death.

This applies even in the case of deliberately false returns, or failure to notify.

The Deceased Tax Cheat

Andrew died on 20 July 2011 and HMRC discover that tax has been lost for the previous ten years as a result of his deliberate failure to return all sources of income.

They can only make assessments for the years 2005/06 to 2010/11 and they must be made before 5 April 2016.

Note that for VAT, the time limit is slightly different – the four-year limit applies from the date of death, but in the case of 'deliberate' wrongdoing the time limit is 20 years – so in Andrew's case, assuming he should have been registered for VAT, the whole ten years before his death can be assessed.

21. 'Protective' Assessments

Because of the time limits explained above (Tips 15 to 20), if HMRC are enquiring into your tax affairs, they will routinely issue assessments for tax years that are about to go out of date for assessment within the normal time limits.

If this happens the important thing is to appeal against the assessment within the 30-day time limit, and ask for collection of the tax to be suspended until the tax investigation has been resolved. HMRC should agree to this without any fuss. Details of how to appeal against such assessments are included in the documents you will be sent with the assessment.

Chapter 4.
Penalties For Lost Tax

22.   Financial Penalties

HMRC have the power to impose numerous types of penalty for mistakes or deliberate errors concerning tax. Most of these penalties are financial, and we will deal with these first, but as we shall see, there are other kinds of penalty that do not involve payment to HMRC.

At the end of a tax investigation, a penalty may be charged, based on the amount of tax that should have been paid but wasn't. This is called the 'potential lost revenue' (PLR).

In most cases, the amount of the PLR is easy to calculate. If you are a 40% taxpayer and you omit income of £1,000 from your tax return, the PLR is £1,000 x 40% = £400.

There can, however, be cases where the PLR arises because of a timing difference. In other words, the tax is paid late rather than not paid at all. The commonest example of this is VAT, where claiming some VAT input tax in (say) the quarter ended 31 March, when you should have claimed it in the following quarter ending 30 June, means that you will have underpaid VAT for the first quarter, but overpaid it for the second quarter when your error reverses itself. In such cases, the PLR is calculated using a notional interest rate of 5%.

Early Claim For VAT

Mr Potter includes VAT input tax of £10,000 in his VAT return for the quarter ending 31 March, but the VAT receipt concerned was received after 31 March and is dated 6 April. Mr Potter should have waited until the next quarter before claiming it, and his VAT return to 31 March therefore understates the VAT payable by £10,000. His next VAT return, however, overstates the VAT due for that quarter by the same amount.

The PLR in this case is £10,000 x 5% x 3/12= £125.

Having established the amount of the PLR, penalties are charged as a percentage of the PLR, based on several factors:

Prompted Disclosure	Mistake despite reasonable care	Careless error	Deliberate inaccuracy	Deliberate inaccuracy with concealment
Maximum	0%	30%	70%	100%
Minimum	0%	15%	35%	50%

Unprompted Disclosure	Mistake despite reasonable care	Careless error	Deliberate inaccuracy	Deliberate inaccuracy with concealment
Maximum	0%	30%	70%	100%
Minimum	0%	0%	20%	30%

These penalties apply to all the taxes you are likely to be concerned with, and they apply to inaccuracies in returns or other tax documents.

Note the difference between the penalties for 'prompted' and 'unprompted' disclosure. Although the maximum penalties are the same, the minimum penalties are significantly lower for 'unprompted' disclosure.

An unprompted disclosure is when you tell HMRC about an error before they ask you, and the lower minimum penalties are there to encourage such behaviour. Once a tax enquiry has begun, it is too late to make an unprompted disclosure, even if HMRC's initial questions were not about the specific item you have got wrong.

As soon as a client tells me they have made an error involving tax, my concern is to make sure this is disclosed to HMRC as quickly as possible, to avoid the risk that HMRC will open an enquiry before we tell them!

Prompted And Unprompted Disclosure

Paul is being investigated by HMRC, because they have discovered (note that word) that he has not been declaring income from the flat in the basement of his house, which he lets out. The undeclared rent, after expenses, amounts to £10,000, and Paul pays income tax at 40%.

He tells his friend Graham about his problems one evening in the pub. Graham, coincidentally, also lets out his basement, and even more coincidentally, the income he omitted from his returns was also £10,000, and he also pays tax at 40%. Graham immediately contacts HMRC and explains that he has failed to declare his rental income.

Both Paul and Graham have 'deliberately' failed to include the rental income in their returns, so in both their cases the maximum penalty will be 70% of the PLR, or £2,800 (£10,000 x 40% = £4,000, times 70% = £2,800).

Assuming however that they both qualify for the minimum penalty – we shall see how they can do this in Tip 23 – Paul will have to pay a penalty of £1,400 (£4,000 x 35%), whereas Graham will only have to pay £800 (£4,000 x 20%).

23. Maximum And Minimum Penalties

As we have seen, the starting point for penalties is how the loss of tax arose – was it a result of careless behaviour, or a deliberate error, and was there then an attempt to conceal that error?

The difference between the maximum and the minimum penalties, however, depends on how the taxpayer behaves during the HMRC enquiry that follows discovery or disclosure of the error.

Having worked out the amount of penalty involved, it is then reduced by percentages for 'telling', 'helping' and 'giving access'.

For example, if there were an unprompted disclosure of a deliberate understatement of income on which the tax was £10,000, the maximum penalty would be £7,000, and the minimum £2,000. The difference between these two is £5,000.

The level of reduction is determined by applying the following percentages to that £5,000:

Up to 30% for 'telling' – that is, admitting to what has been done and explaining how it happened. The reduction here could be up to £1,500 (30% of £5,000).

Up to 40% for 'helping' – by answering all HMRC's questions and providing all the necessary information to quantify the tax lost. This could reduce the penalty by a further £2,000.

Up to 30% for 'access' – such as getting copies of bank statements from the bank if necessary, allowing HMRC to see any documentation, and so on. This is worth up to £1,500 in the example we are looking at.

The key point is that you will significantly increase the penalties if you are obstructive or refuse to admit anything is wrong until the last moment, but you can also dramatically reduce the penalty by cooperating.

We shall revisit the significance of 'telling', 'helping' and 'giving access' in Chapter 10, when we look at some case studies.

24.   Suspended Penalties

In some cases, having worked out the level of penalty that is appropriate, HMRC will agree to 'suspend' it. **This only applies to penalties for 'careless' mistakes in returns, not to 'deliberate' errors, and in order for a penalty to be suspended, the taxpayer has first to agree that he or she has been careless.**

If a penalty is suspended, this means it is not paid immediately. Instead, a period (not longer than two years) is agreed with the taxpayer, and so are the conditions for the suspension.

The conditions set are such that if they are followed, then the careless error will not occur again.

Assuming the conditions are met during the suspension period, then the suspended penalty will be cancelled and there will be nothing to pay.

It is *always* worth asking about suspended penalties in cases of careless error. HMRC officers are required to consider such requests carefully, and in my experience *every* request I have made for a client's penalty for careless inaccuracy to be suspended has been agreed.

Examples of suspended penalties

- A client omitted a significant amount of investment income from his return. This occurred because he had recently received a large lump sum on retirement, and the bank with which he had invested it had given him incorrect information. The penalty was suspended until the following February (to cover the period during which his next tax return would be filed), and (in addition to the condition that all tax returns and tax payments be made on time, which applies to every suspended penalty) the condition was that he obtain full details of his investments with the bank concerned and check them before submitting the next return.

- Another client claimed input VAT in the quarter before he should have done – he knew the amount of VAT involved in a specific purchase of materials, but he had not received a VAT receipt for it. The penalty was suspended for three months (until the next VAT return) on condition that return claimed the correct amount of input tax.

- For several years, a client had not been earning enough money to be required to make repayments of his student loan. By the time his income reached the level where such repayments were required, he had forgotten he needed to include the loan repayments in his return (he was self-employed, so there was no employer to deduct the repayments). The penalty was suspended until his next return was filed, on condition he included the student loan repayment this time.

In all the above cases, the conditions were met and the penalties were cancelled.

25.   Failure To Notify Chargeability

If you are liable to pay tax – income tax, CGT, or corporation tax if you are a company, and you have not been sent a notice to file a return, you have an obligation to notify HMRC that you are liable to tax and need to file a return. You must do this within six months of the end of the tax year in which you became liable to the tax concerned if you are an individual, or within 12 months from the end of the relevant accounting period if you are a company.

There are similar time limits for other taxes (for example, for VAT you are required to notify HMRC and register within one month of your turnover for the previous 12 months exceeding the VAT threshold).

The penalties for failure to notify are based on the same percentages as those for inaccuracies – see Tip 22 for details. The level of penalty will depend on whether the failure was deliberate, deliberate and concealed, or 'non-deliberate', which is the equivalent of 'careless' in the table for inaccuracy penalties.

Examples of non-deliberate, deliberate, and deliberate and concealed failure to notify – again, from HMRC's own manuals:

Example of non-deliberate failure to notify

Mark is employed as a bus driver. He is not issued notices to make a self assessment return. An aunt leaves him £80,000 in her will. He puts the money on deposit in the bank while he decides what to do with it. The bank deducts income tax from the interest at basic rate. Part of his income now falls into the higher rate band and therefore he has an additional tax liability which he fails to notify to HMRC. In view of Mark's apparent knowledge and experience you accept that he was not aware that he was liable to pay more tax. His failure is non-deliberate.

Example of deliberate failure to notify

Susan is employed as a consultant engineer but also does freelance work. Susan knows that as she does not receive SA returns she must notify us that she also has income from self-employment. She decides not to do so. She has deliberately chosen not to notify her liability to income tax but has not taken any steps to conceal the need to notify us of her self-employment.

Example of deliberate and concealed failure to notify

Thomas has not made any tax returns. You find that he acquired a property in 2012 from which he receives rental income and has failed to notify chargeability for 2012-13 onwards. When you ask about the source of the funds used to purchase the property, Thomas says the money was loaned to him by overseas family members. You later find that Thomas owned a number of rental properties before 2012 and that the money actually came from the sale of one of those properties. Thomas has deliberately failed to notify his liability for all years. For the earlier years, when asked to explain the source of his funds, Thomas took active steps to conceal his liability. For those years, the failure is therefore deliberate and concealed.

Just as there is no penalty for an error in a return if you have taken 'reasonable care' there is no penalty for failing to notify if you have a 'reasonable excuse'.

We have briefly looked at 'reasonable excuses' in Tip 9, and you will recall that bereavement, sudden illness and natural disasters were just about the only examples of a 'reasonable excuse'. Simply not knowing you should notify HMRC is not a reasonable excuse – see the example of Mark the bus driver above.

It is generally quite unlikely that you will have a reasonable excuse for not notifying HMRC that you are chargeable to tax.

26. Penalties For Inadequate Business Records

We have seen that HMRC have the power to 'inspect' your business records. If they find they are not adequate for the purpose of producing the relevant tax returns, they can impose a penalty of up to £500 (£250 for businesses in their first year of trading), and further penalties of up to a total of £3,000 can be imposed.

The question of what business records are required is a difficult one. Except in the case of corporation tax and VAT where there are specific detailed requirements as to what records are required, the test is really whether the records kept are adequate to enable a proper set of accounts to be drawn up. The records required will also vary according to the size and complexity of the business. In most cases, a businessperson will keep the appropriate records in any case, because he or she needs to know how the business is doing.

These penalties also apply if you fail to keep the records for the required periods, which are:

- for personal tax returns – the first anniversary of the 31 January filing date;
- for a person running a business – the fifth anniversary of the filing date – or for a limited company or a partnership, the sixth anniversary of the end of the accounting period.

There are further penalties (of up to £3,000) if you destroy records during a tax enquiry, but in practice such a (stupid) action would probably be dealt with by denying the reductions in the main penalty for 'helping' and 'giving access'.

27.   Offshore Penalties

The percentage rates for penalties for inaccuracy or for failure to notify (and for late returns – see below) are increased if the tax involved relates to income or gains arising outside the UK.

The amount of the increase depends on which of three categories the offshore jurisdiction falls into.

- Category 1 territories – no increase.
- Category 2 territories – multiply penalty by 1.5.
- Category 3 territories – double the penalty.

The countries in Categories 1 and 3 are as follows. Any other country is, by default, in Category 2.

Category 1

Anguilla	Germany	New Zealand
Aruba	Greece	(not including Tokelau)
Australia	Guernsey	Norway
Belgium	Hungary	Poland
Bulgaria	Ireland	Portugal
Canada	Isle of Man	Romania
Cayman Islands	Italy	Slovakia
Cyprus	Japan	Slovenia
Czech Republic	Korea, South	Spain
Denmark (not including Faroe Islands and Greenland)	Latvia	Sweden
	Lithuania	United States of America (not including overseas territories and possessions)
	Malta	
Estonia	Montserrat	
Finland	Netherlands (not including Bonaire, Sint Eustatius and Saba)	
France		

Category 3

Albania	Dominica	Nicaragua
Algeria	Dominican Republic	Niue
Andorra	Ecuador	Palau
Antigua and Barbuda	El Salvador	Panama
Armenia	Gabon	Paraguay
Bahrain	Grenada	Peru
Barbados	Guatemala	Saint Kitts and Nevis
Belize	Honduras	Saint Lucia
Bonaire, Sint Eustatius and Saba	Iran	Saint Vincent and the Grenadines
	Iraq	
Brazil	Jamaica	San Marino
Cameroon	Kyrgyzstan	Seychelles
Cape Verde	Lebanon	Sint Maarten
Colombia	Macau	Suriname
Congo, Republic of the	Marshall Islands	Syria
Cook Islands	Mauritius	Tokelau
Costa Rica	Micronesia, Federated States of	Tonga
Curaçao		Trinidad and Tobago
Cuba	Monaco	United Arab Emirates
Democratic People's Republic of Korea	Nauru	Uruguay

28. Penalties For Late Returns And Payments Of Tax

If you are late in filing a return (whether for self assessment, VAT, or any of the other taxes), then you may become liable for a penalty. This area of tax penalties is still in the process of evolving, and not all the legislation is in place yet, but for the purposes of this book we will concentrate on penalties for late filing of an individual's self assessment for income tax or CGT.

Generally speaking, the filing date for a self assessment return is 31 January (if you file online), and the penalties for missing this are as follows:

Length Of Delay	Penalty You Will Have To Pay
1 day late	A penalty of £100. This applies even if you have no tax to pay or have paid the tax you owe.
3 months late	£10 for each following day — up to a 90-day maximum of £900. This is as well as the fixed penalty above.
6 months late	£300 or 5% of the tax due, whichever is the higher. This is as well as the penalties above.
12 months late	£300 or 5% of the tax due, whichever is the higher. In serious cases you may be asked to pay up to 100% of the tax due instead. These are as well as the penalties above.

Even if you have filed your return on time, there are also penalties for late payment of the tax, depending on how late you are in paying:

Length Of Delay	Penalty You Will Have To Pay
30 days late	5% of the tax you owe at that date.
6 months late	5% of the tax you owe at that date. This is as well as the 5% above.
12 months late	5% of the tax unpaid at that date. This is as well as the two 5% penalties above.

Note that these penalties only apply to the main payment due on 31 January, not to the payments on account due on 31 January and 31 July.

Late Payment Penalties

Charles' tax for the 2014/15 tax year is due on 31 January 2016, but he doesn't pay it until 5 August 2016.

It is over six months late so he will have to pay all of the following:

- 5% of the tax unpaid at 2 March (30 days after the date the tax was due);
- 5% of the tax unpaid at 2 August (five months after the first penalty); and
- interest on all outstanding amounts, including any unpaid penalties.

29. Non-Financial Penalties – Name And Shame

HMRC have always been able to publicise the results of their criminal prosecutions for tax fraud and other offences, but since the 2009 Finance Act they have also had the power to publish the names of 'deliberate tax defaulters'.

This means those who have deliberately underpaid their tax and been charged a penalty of at least £25,000. Note that anyone who has earned the maximum reduction in his or her penalties for telling, helping, and giving access cannot be published on the list – yet another example of the importance of cooperation.

The details that can be published are:

- the name of the person who incurs the penalty including any trading name, previous name or pseudonym;
- the person's address (or registered office, in the case of a company);
- the nature of any business carried on by the person;
- the amount of the qualifying relevant penalty or penalties;
- the qualifying potential lost revenue (PLR) in relation to the qualifying relevant penalty, or the total of the qualifying PLR for all of the qualifying relevant penalties;
- the periods when the inaccuracy, failure or wrongdoing that gave rise to the qualifying relevant penalty or penalties occurred; and
- any other details that HMRC considers necessary in order to make the person's identity clear.

It is not entirely clear what HMRC hopes to gain from publishing this information, and indeed they only published the first names in February 2013, which seems to indicate a certain lack of enthusiasm.

30. Non-Financial Penalties – The 'Managing Serious Defaulters Programme'

The 'managing serious defaulters programme' was first launched under a slightly different name in 2011, but has more recently been extended and re-launched. It is essentially a much more onerous compliance regime, and applies to those charged penalties for 'deliberate' inaccuracies as well as to those convicted of more serious, criminal, tax offences.

If they are included in the programme, the taxpayers concerned may be subject to any or all of the following:

- unannounced visits;
- enquiries into every return submitted;
- requests for additional information.

It is important to realise that there is no appeal against inclusion in the programme, because all HMRC are doing is using their regular powers, and the only way to get out of it is to persuade HMRC that you have changed your ways. HMRC claim that, in most cases, this will take between two and five years.

As well as the obvious inconvenience and expense of complying with all of HMRC's demands, inclusion in the programme would be a huge handicap to a businessperson, because, for example, if they were to become a partner in a different business or a director of a different company, that partnership or company may also be included in the programme.

It is not clear how many taxpayers are included in the programme, but for obvious reasons it is most important that you avoid becoming one of them!

31. Penalties For Dishonest Tax Agents

If a tax agent is found to have been dishonest in his or her dealings with HMRC – for example, by deliberately omitting income from a client's tax returns, or encouraging other forms of tax evasion, then the agent will be liable to a penalty of between £5,000 and £50,000.

As this only applies to those who deal with HMRC on behalf of their clients, you may think it is not relevant to you, but it can be another example of a penalty for you too.

Quite recently, a number of local businesses that used the services of a certain tax adviser were subjected to tax enquiries, because HMRC discovered that the adviser had deliberately falsified their accounts and returns in order to reduce the tax they paid.

If your tax adviser ever gets into trouble with HMRC, it can have a knock-on effect on you!

32. 'Special Reduction' Of Penalties

The penalty regime as set out above is quite rigid – essentially, the level of penalty depends on:

- the 'potential lost revenue' (PLR);
- whether the error was careless, deliberate, or deliberate with concealment;
- whether the disclosure was prompted or unprompted; and
- whether the taxpayer cooperated in settling the matter.

Based on the above facts, the amount of the penalty is calculated within quite narrow guidelines.

In some circumstances, there is scope for HMRC to make further reductions in penalties in cases where 'uncommon or exceptional' circumstances mean that the strictly calculated penalty is not appropriate.

This is very unusual, and it is a decision that can only be taken by HMRC's Central Policy Unit after a referral from the inspector dealing with the case.

An example given by HMRC is a case where a father and son are in partnership, and when the father retires, the son omits to change their VAT registration to that of sole trader.

Technically speaking, there may be significant amounts of PLR, because the VAT paid under the now invalid partnership registration was no longer due, and nor should the partnership have reclaimed input VAT, but assuming the correct amounts of VAT have in fact been paid at the right time, it would be unjust to exact the possibly large penalty arrived at using the normal rules. A 'special reduction' might therefore be made.

In practice, 'special reductions' have been applied in cases where the way the penalty regime operates produces obviously unjust results. It is unusual to see a special reduction – and unlikely that you will qualify for one!

33.   New Penalties

At the time of writing (May 2015) HMRC are consulting on major changes to the penalty regime. It is likely that the changes will result in a more complex system for calculating penalties, with more emphasis on the 'behaviour' of the taxpayer, and (on the bright side!) more tolerance for simple mistakes, particularly in a case where it is the first time there has been a problem.

34.   HMRC's Worrying Proposals

There have also been other, more worrying proposals, including:

- A 'strict liability' criminal offence of undeclared offshore income (at present some taxpayers have pleaded ignorance of the rules to avoid prosecution – 'strict liability' would remove this defence).
- Increased penalties, possibly based on the amount of money held offshore.
- Civil penalties for those who assist in tax evasion.
- Criminal penalties for companies who allow evasion to take place.

Chapter 5.
Disclosure

35.   Contacting HMRC

I have already explained the importance (in terms of the level of penalty) of disclosing any tax irregularities before HMRC ask you about your tax affairs.

In normal circumstances, the best way to go about this is to approach a competent tax adviser (more about these valuable individuals later) and seek his or her advice.

The tax adviser will (or should) arrange for a letter to be sent to HMRC disclosing in general terms what is wrong, to be followed up as soon as possible by a more detailed summary of the income omitted, or the tax otherwise unpaid. This should secure you the 'unprompted disclosure' rates of penalty.

There are, however, certain circumstances in which a more formal approach is appropriate.

36.   Other HMRC Campaigns

As well as the offshore programmes, HMRC have run a series of campaigns since 2007, aimed at specific UK targets. Past examples include plumbers, medical professionals, e-traders, direct sellers, and electricians.

At the time of writing there are three of these campaigns up and running:

- The Credit Card Sales campaign (disclosure of business sales by credit card)
- The Second Incomes Campaign (disclosure of 'moonlighting' income by employees)
- The Let Property Campaign (disclosure of undeclared rental income)

and there will no doubt be others in future.

These campaigns are usually regionally based, and involve:

- identifying a target group;
- offering an opportunity to make a disclosure on simple terms and at fixed penalty rates; and
- using information and research to follow up and target those who do not take advantage of the campaign.

If you become aware that there is a current campaign that could include you, it would be most unwise not to participate.

Not only do you now know that your business sector is a specific target, but if you do not sign up and are subsequently discovered, you are likely to suffer a higher rate of penalty than otherwise, as HMRC might well argue that ignoring the campaign moved your tax default from 'careless' to 'deliberate'.

37. The Contractual Disclosure Facility (CDF)

The Contractual Disclosure Facility (CDF) applies in cases where HMRC suspect that criminal fraud may have been committed in relation to someone's tax affairs. They will send you a letter enclosing a copy of Code of Practice 9 and a form to sign up to the CDF.

At this point, you have three choices, and you have 60 days to decide:

- Sign the form offering to make a CDF, and follow it up within a further 60 days with full details of the fraud. If you do this, you are guaranteed not to be prosecuted for a criminal offence in connection with the fraud.
- Sign the alternative form you will find in the letter, denying any wrongdoing. HMRC will still investigate, but if they find fraud they may prosecute you for criminal offences.
- Do nothing, in which case the result will be the same as the second bullet point.

Unless you are absolutely certain you are not guilty of fraud, the only realistic course of action is the first.

If you receive a COP 9/CDF letter, it is absolutely essential to seek advice from a specialist in tax investigations immediately. Even the letter from HMRC contains their advice to seek professional help!

38. Offshore Disclosure Facilities

Given the potentially higher rates of penalties for tax lost on offshore income or gains, it is worth checking to see if you qualify for any of these special facilities. At the time of writing, there are special terms available for those who need to disclose income or gains arising in the following jurisdictions:

- Isle of Man;

- Guernsey;

- Jersey;

- Lichtenstein;

- Switzerland.

The first four of these offer very similar terms – essentially:

- a fixed penalty of 10% on tax for years up to 2007/08;

- a fixed penalty of 20% on tax for later years;

- tax collected to be limited to periods beginning on or after 1 April 1999 (so in practice, the tax year 1999/2000) – note that there are exceptions to this; and

- Must sign up for the Crown Dependency and Lichtenstein facilities before 31 December 2015.

The Lichtenstein facility is the Rolls Royce of the offshore disclosure facilities. It has the same fixed penalty rates, but it also allows the taxpayer to elect to use a flat rate of 40% tax to cover ALL tax that might be due – including, for example, inheritance tax that might apply in the case of certain types of trust.

The Lichtenstein facility will end on 31 December 2015, to be replaced with a much more severe regime including higher penalties (minimum 30%) and no automatic immunity from prosecution.

No finish date has yet been set for the Swiss facility.

It is possible to make yourself eligible for any of these disclosure facilities even if you do not have an account in the relevant country, by opening an account there.

The advantage of this is that the terms of the disclosure facility cover all tax unpaid for the period concerned, not just that in the foreign jurisdiction, so for example it could cover UK income tax on undeclared business profits.

The detailed conditions and rules for these disclosure facilities are extremely complex, and it is essential to get good professional advice if you think they could apply to you.

These disclosure facilities are all part of an HMRC programme to stamp out offshore tax evasion – another aspect of the programme is the one-off levy of between 21% and 41% of the balance (yes, the balance, not the income!) on Swiss bank accounts that were open on 31 December 2010 and were still open on 31 May 2013.

This applies to all accounts held by UK residents where they have not provided the bank with a 'Certificate of Tax Compliance' issued by HMRC. It will be followed by an annual withholding tax of up to 48% on the income from these accounts.

Chapter 6.
Tax Avoidance, Tax Evasion, And Tax Fraud

39. 'The Thickness Of A Prison Wall'

'The thickness of a prison wall' was the answer given by a past Chancellor of the Exchequer when asked the difference between tax avoidance and tax evasion.

The distinction is an important one, because whereas tax avoidance is legal, tax evasion is a criminal offence, and often involves tax fraud.

The problem is that some schemes marketed as tax avoidance are in fact dangerously close to tax fraud, and I have come across several examples of taxpayers being sold a 'tax planning' scheme by an adviser that was in fact fraudulent.

The best defence against this is to use the services of a reputable tax adviser, but as a rule of thumb, any scheme claimed to be tax avoidance that relies on HMRC not being given the full facts is probably tax evasion.

40. Spotlights

HMRC publish a series called 'Spotlights' which highlights specific tax avoidance schemes they believe do not work, and as part of this section of their website they offer some rules of thumb for spotting tax avoidance schemes that might tip over into tax evasion, or simply might not work.

Whilst I do not agree entirely with everything on their list, it is worth reproducing here as it gives an insight into HMRC's own views on the subject:

Tax planning to be wary of

- *It sounds too good to be true.*
- *Artificial or contrived arrangements are involved.*
- *It seems very complex given what you want to do.*
- *There are guaranteed returns with apparently no risk.*
- *There are secrecy or confidentiality agreements.*
- *Upfront fees are payable or the arrangement is on a no win/no fee basis.*
- *The scheme is said to be vetted by a top lawyer or accountant but no details of their opinion are provided.*
- *The scheme is said to be approved by HMRC (it does not follow that this is true).*
- *Taxation of income is delayed or tax deductions accelerated.*
- *Tax benefits are disproportionate to the commercial activity.*
- *Offshore companies or trusts are involved for no sound commercial reason.*
- *The involvement of professional trustees is claimed to guarantee that the arrangements succeed.*

- *A tax haven or banking secrecy country is involved without any sound commercial reason.*
- *Tax exempt entities, such as pension funds, are involved inappropriately.*
- *It contains exit arrangements designed to sidestep tax consequences.*
- *It involves money going in a circle back to where it started.*
- *Low risk loans to be paid off by future earnings are involved.*
- *The scheme promoter lends the funding needed.*
- *There is a requirement to take out insurance against the failure of the tax planning to deliver the tax benefits.*

It would be extremely unwise to use a specific tax avoidance scheme that has been highlighted in Spotlights, because it will certainly cause you to be the subject of a tax enquiry, and in some cases HMRC may argue that by using such a scheme when they had already told you through Spotlights that it does not work represents being 'careless' with your tax liability.

They have certainly threatened to do this, though I have yet to hear of them actually seeking penalties in such a case.

41. Disclosure Of Tax Avoidance Schemes (DOTAS)

The tax legislation requires those who promote tax avoidance schemes to register them with HMRC. There are rules defining what sort of schemes have to be registered, and in some cases a scheme will escape from the requirement to be registered – for example most (but not all) schemes in existence when the Disclosure of Tax Avoidance Schemes (DOTAS) rules were brought in are exempt from registration – this is known as 'grandfathering'.

You should, however, be very cautious if you are told that the scheme you are being sold is exempt from registration, as there are penalties if the scheme should have been registered and has not been.

If you use a DOTAS scheme, you will be given a registration number for it, and it is compulsory to include this number on your self assessment return – there is a space on Page 4 of the 'Additional Information' pages. There is a penalty of £100 for failing to do so, rising to £500 and £1,000 if two or three schemes are involved.

It is important to realise that the fact that a scheme has a DOTAS number does not mean HMRC have approved it or that they agree it works – most of the schemes highlighted in Spotlights (see Tip 40) are registered under DOTAS.

42. What Will Happen If I Use A Tax Avoidance Scheme?

You will not be surprised to learn that having a DOTAS registration number on your tax return greatly increases the chances of being the subject of a tax investigation!

Generally speaking, investigations into tax avoidance schemes are conducted centrally, led by HMRC's Anti-Avoidance Group, who will deal with the promoters of the scheme.

The aim will be to either reach agreement, or to arrange for an example of the scheme in question to be heard by the Tax Tribunal (and probably the higher courts as well) to determine if it works or not.

In many cases, the fee you will have paid for taking part in the scheme will include the costs of arguing with HMRC about the scheme.

An investigation into a tax avoidance scheme is unlike most other tax enquiries because the individual users of the scheme will not be much involved in the process. You are unlikely to get many letters from HMRC, after the first one that tells you formally that your tax return is going to be investigated because of the tax avoidance scheme.

After that, the negotiations will be conducted with the scheme promoters, and they can drag on for a number of years. In some cases, HMRC will write to you with an offer to close down the enquiry into your return if you agree to some sort of compromise. Typically, the promoter will also keep you informed of the progress of the dispute.

43.   Should I Use Tax Avoidance Schemes?

There has been a lot of mostly ill-informed criticism of tax avoidance by international companies, and the current political climate seems very hostile to tax avoidance. Does this mean you should not use tax avoidance schemes?

I do not believe there is a moral issue here, but you need to be very cautious if you are offered a tax avoidance scheme.

- Make sure the promoter is a reputable one and that the scheme is legal – I mean legal in the sense that it does not cross the line into tax evasion. If in doubt, consult an independent tax adviser.
- Make sure you are clear about the fees to be charged – some schemes involve an annual fee to run the scheme as well as the upfront fee, and make sure you will not be required to contribute to the costs of any litigation after you have paid the fee for the scheme.
- Realise that you are likely to be in for a number of years of uncertainty – five years is not an unusual timescale – before you will know for sure whether the scheme has worked.

Tax avoidance schemes are not for everyone – you need to have a certain sort of mentality to take the stress of a long argument with HMRC. As one of my clients said when he told me he had turned down an avoidance scheme that was offered to him, 'I'd rather sleep at night!'

44. Will HMRC Be More Likely To Investigate My Tax Returns If I Use A Tax Avoidance Scheme?

If you use a tax avoidance scheme, you will be by definition a high earner, and as such you are already considered a bigger risk than many other taxpayers by HMRC, but the short answer is yes – if you are involved in a tax avoidance scheme this will increase the chances of HMRC investigating your tax returns – even in years when you are not using any specific avoidance schemes.

45.   The General Anti-Abuse Rule

Another new weapon for tackling tax avoidance is the 'General Anti-Abuse Rule', or GAAR. Essentially this says that where a tax planning scheme clearly tries to flout the legislation by producing a result clearly not intended by the law, HMRC can charge tax as if the avoidance scheme had not been used.

The theory is that this will only be used in the most extreme cases, but it is having a significant deterrent effect on tax planning. I was recently at a meeting where a clever but (to my mind, at least) perfectly reasonable and innocent tax planning idea was discussed, and it was decided to take Counsel's opinion on whether it would be caught by the GAAR before implementing it.

46. Accelerated Payment Notices

One of the attractions of tax avoidance schemes used to be the fact that even if they eventually did not work, they had the effect of deferring payment of the tax concerned for several years, at the cost of only (currently) 3% interest.

HMRC now have the power, in cases involving DOTAS or the GAAR, to require that the tax in dispute be paid up front, to be repaid if the taxpayer wins his or her case. This has removed a major attraction of avoidance schemes.

47.   Follower Notices

Once again, in cases involving DOTAS or the GAAR, if HMRC win a case involving another taxpayer but which they consider involves the same legal issues as your dispute with them, they can issue you a 'follower notice' requiring you to amend your return to reflect the decision of the court in the other case. If you do not do this and you eventually lose, there are penalties of up to 50% of the tax involved.

48.   New Closure Rules

There is currently a consultation process going on over another proposal – that HMRC should be able to take one aspect of a case to the Tax Tribunal and get a ruling on that aspect, without having the rest of the matters in dispute heard. The point of this is that tax avoidance schemes are often extremely complex and involve numerous points of interpretation. This has led to long delays in getting the whole case ready for a Tribunal hearing.

The unfair aspect of the proposed change is that it will apply only to HMRC, not to the taxpayer on the other side of the argument!

Chapter 7.
The Rules Of The Game – How Tax Enquiries Should Be Conducted

49.   The Opening Letter Or The Visit?

The way HMRC begins an enquiry will depend on the taxes they are looking at. In the case of income tax, capital gains tax and corporation tax, an enquiry will almost always begin with a letter.

In the case of VAT, PAYE, and deductions under the Construction Industry Scheme, it is more common to begin by arranging to visit the business premises – though the request for a visit may itself be in the form of a letter.

50. Beware Of The Informal Approach!

There is an increasing tendency for tax inspectors to try to begin enquiries on an 'informal' basis, perhaps by asking to have a telephone discussion about the return of accounts they are looking at. It is very much a matter of judgement how to respond to such requests, but on the whole I do not recommend agreeing to this.

If you are contacted in this way you should refer the inspector to your tax adviser (and if you have not got one, you should get one!).

If I am approached informally by an inspector about one of my clients, I will normally ask him to put his concerns and requests for information in writing, and also to formally open an enquiry by giving the appropriate statutory notice.

It may seem odd that I want a formal enquiry to be opened, but the reason is simple – it is to protect my client. Only once an enquiry has been formally opened do the 'reasonably required' rules described in Chapter 3 start to apply.

Why Not To Agree To An Informal Approach

I received a phone call from a tax inspector about one of my clients, and he raised three issues relating to the latest set of accounts for the company concerned.

One of them concerned 'transfer pricing', which refers to the rules governing the prices charged between companies that are controlled by the same person.

I was pretty sure that he had no right to ask these questions (the rules for transfer pricing do not apply to all companies), but rather than argue about it on the phone – thus potentially not being cooperative – I asked him to formally open an enquiry and put his questions in writing.

Once he had done this I was able to write back with the information he had asked for in connection with the other two issues, and saying that because the transfer pricing rules did not apply in this case, the information he had asked for under this heading was not 'reasonably required' for the purposes of 'checking the tax position' of my client. The inspector reluctantly agreed.

51. A Typical Opening Letter

A letter opening a tax enquiry will begin by stating that the inspector has decided to enquire into your tax return for the year, and will refer to the relevant legislation (in the case of a self assessment return, section 9A of the 1970 Taxes Management Act).

If the enquiry is an 'aspect' enquiry (see Tip 3) the letter will then explain the specific points the inspector wishes to check, and should contain some sort of assurance that if the questions on these points can be satisfactorily dealt with, he or she will not be checking any other points in the return.

Example Of An Aspect Enquiry Opening Letter

The opening letter asked for the following information:

- Detailed computations of the (large) claim for capital allowances.
- An analysis of the (large) deduction claimed for repairs.
- Further information about a provisional claim to 'roll over' a capital gain.

We provided the information on capital allowances and repairs, and explained why the information on the rollover claim was not 'reasonably required'.

A couple of weeks later the inspector wrote back confirming he had closed down his enquiry and no amendments were required to the tax return.

If the letter does not contain assurances about only checking specific points, but asks for a lot of information about the entries on the return, then this means the enquiry is a 'full' enquiry.

52. A Typical 'Full' Enquiry – Request For Records And Information

Normally, a 'full' enquiry will relate to a business, and the opening letter will ask to see the business records as well as posing a number of questions about the business.

Note that you are required to give the inspector access to the business records, but in the case of a large business it may be more appropriate for him or her to visit your premises to inspect them.

Many businesses these days use computerised records, and HMRC are also entitled to access to these, but you will want to have someone who understands the software to make sure that access is restricted to the business records alone.

53.   A Typical Full Enquiry – Meeting

Once you send in the business records or you have answered the various questions the next stage, which will typically follow a month or so after you have sent your reply, will be for the inspector to ask for a meeting.

Inspectors like to give the impression that it is compulsory to attend these meetings, but it is not, and they have no power to force you to go to a meeting with them.

If you have nothing to hide or if you have found some mistakes and you want to disclose them to HMRC a meeting is often the best way to do it – though it is absolutely essential that you have a professional adviser with you when you go to the meeting.

It may seem expensive to pay an adviser's hourly rate to accompany you to a meeting with the inspector, but it will usually be money well spent. Your adviser will try to ensure that your side of the matter is properly put before the inspector, and he or she should protect you from some of the questions you are likely to be asked.

Under the stress of a meeting like this, you will probably feel that you want to appear as helpful as possible to the inspector, and all too often I have seen cases where this led to people making up the answers to questions when the truth was that they didn't know the correct answer.

Here are a few examples, together with their hidden traps:

Q: How much cash do you normally have in your possession, in your pocket or in the house? What is the largest amount you have

had, and when did you have it? Don't get this wrong – you may later be confronted with a 'cash test'. This typically only applies to businesses with significant cash takings – pubs and taxi drivers, for example. Essentially, it involves comparing cash income declared and cash drawn from the bank with cash banked and cash spent. If you have either banked or spent more cash than you have either received as business takings or drawn from the bank, the inference is of course that you have not declared all the cash income received!

Q: Who takes the kids to school? Would that be you, in the van that you 'only use for business'?

Q: What do you do in your spare time? If you try to give the impression that you stay in every night, you may look rather foolish when your subscription to the yacht club shows up in your cheque stubs! In one of my cases, I found payments for a number of flying lessons in the bank account of a man who 'had no hobbies' and 'never went out'.

Q: Do you bank all the cash you receive? This leads back to the cash test referred to already.

After the meeting the inspector will send you his or her notes of the meeting. The inspector will invite you to sign them to confirm you agree with them.

Most advisers including myself say that you should not agree to sign the notes because once you have done so it is difficult to argue later that there are mistakes in them. The inspector will try to find discrepancies between what you have said and what is in the records.

There is also a certain tendency amongst inspectors to record what they wish had been said rather than what actually was said. It is very important to read those notes through carefully and to challenge immediately anything that you consider to be inaccurate.

In some cases I advise people not to go to a meeting at all. This is typically where I don't think that the client would show up very well at the meeting, perhaps because he or she is somewhat paranoid and nervous, or perhaps because I can't trust the client to keep their temper!

It is perfectly possible to insist on dealing with things through correspondence with the inspector, though the problem with this approach is that it takes a lot longer and potentially it is more expensive for the client in terms of the adviser's time.

Provided that you and your adviser agree on this approach and it isn't going to be to your disadvantage, then go to the meeting.

After the meeting, as well as the notes, the inspector will possibly come up with more questions or may actually make a proposal as to how to settle the matter. The inspector may even agree to settle without any alterations to the figures but more typically he or she will propose some additions to the profits.

54. Negotiations

Your tax adviser will then negotiate with the inspector, which can last some time before finally the investigation is closed. A good adviser will balance the desire to fight every point with the need to settle things in a cost-effective manner.

Once it has been agreed:

- either there are no changes needed to the accounts, or
- what those changes are,

the time has come for making a settlement with HMRC and paying any of the additional tax that is due.

I would be amazed if this type of investigation lasted less than six months; I would also be amazed if it lasted longer than two years.

In fact in most cases an investigation lasting longer than two years would suggest to me that the adviser isn't doing his or her job properly. A good adviser should be able to put pressure on the inspector to negotiate in a constructive manner – in the last resort, where the inspector has found little of significance but won't let go, the taxpayer can appeal to the First-tier Tribunal – see Tip 75 – to force the inspector to close down the enquiry.

55. Closure Notices

At the end of a tax enquiry, the inspector will issue a 'closure notice' formally closing it down. It is, however, also open to the taxpayer to apply to the Tax Tribunal for them to issue a closure notice. This action – or the threat of it – may be necessary in cases where the inspector cannot seem to make up his or her mind about whether to continue the enquiry or not.

In addition to the closure notice, if anything has been found to be amiss, you are likely to be asked to complete and sign three documents:

- Statement of Assets and Liabilities (Tip 56);
- Letter of Offer (Tip 57);
- Certificate of Full Disclosure (Tip 58).

56.   Statement Of Assets And Liabilities

A Statement of Assets and Liabilities is what the name implies, and is a summary of all your assets and liabilities at the current time. Its main purpose is to confirm that the picture of your income that has emerged as a result of the investigation is consistent with your actual wealth.

57.   Letter Of Offer

A Letter of Offer will be used in cases where HMRC are going to charge you penalties for the errors they have discovered.

A typical Letter of Offer will be worded like this:

TO THE COMMISSIONERS FOR HER MAJESTY'S REVENUE AND CUSTOMS

The tax [and the Class 4 National Insurance Contributions]* on the statement[s]* [below/attached/overleaf]* [is/are]* unpaid, wholly or in part, because of my failure to meet all my obligations under the Taxes Acts. On the basis that no proceedings are taken against me for [that tax/Class 4 NIC]* [those liabilities]*, or for the penalties, surcharge and interest on [it/them]*

I ....
      [insert name of the taxpayer]

Of ....
      [insert address]

offer the sum of   £..............

less   £..............   which I have already paid.

The balance of   £..............   will be paid within .... days of the date
                                         of your letter accepting this offer.

If the full sum has not been paid by that day, interest at the rate which applies for Section 86 Taxes Management Act 1970 which may be varied from time to time, will also be payable on any unpaid balance from that day. This interest will be payable without deduction of tax and shall not be claimed or allowed as a deduction in computing any income, profits or losses for any tax purposes.

[This offer includes the additional interest on the increase to the amounts of the payments on account for the year ..../........]*

Signed.. Date ....

Statement of Income Tax*/Capital Gains Tax*/and National Insurance Contributions*

[use for SA years]

Year	Amount £

Statement of Duties unpaid by me*

[use for pre SA years included]

Year	Nature of Duty	Amount £

Statement of Class 4 National Insurance Contributions unpaid by me*

Year	Amount £

The following details are for HMRC's purposes only and do not form part of this offer.

Reference number:	User to insert either LC post reference or Caseflow reference

[Delete as appropriate, remove **square** brackets and words in italics. Ensure the end result is correct, logical and good English.]*

58.   Certificate Of Full Disclosure

A Certificate of Full Disclosure reads like this:

CERTIFICATE OF FULL DISCLOSURE

TO: HM REVENUE & CUSTOMS: SPECIAL CIVIL INVESTIGATIONS/CIVIL INVESTIGATION OF FRAUD TEAM

I ....

of ....

HEREBY CERTIFY that to the best of my knowledge and belief, I have made a complete disclosure to you of:-

1   all banking accounts (whether current or deposit, business or private), all savings and loan accounts, deposit receipts, and Building and Co-operative Society accounts:-

(a)   which stand or at any time have stood in my own name or in the name of any business with which I have been concerned,

(b)   in which I am or have been interested or in which I have or have had power to operate or control, jointly or solely,

        which are in existence now or which have existed at any time during the period from   to   .

2   all assets of whatever description or wherever kept (including Savings Certificates, Premium Bonds, life assurance policies, cash in hand, jewellery, furnishings and other valuables) which I or any business with which I have been concerned, now possess or have possessed at any time during the period from   to .

3   all gifts, whether in cash or in any other form, made by me to children or to other persons during the period from   to   .

4   all sources of income not indicated in (1) and (2) above, and the amounts of income derived therefrom, and all facts bearing upon my liability to Direct Taxes, Indirect Taxes, and allied taxes in the period from   to   inclusive.

5   all facts bearing upon the liabilities of   and any other business with which I have been concerned from   to   inclusive.

The amount of my own cash in hand at the present date does not exceed £   .

The bank and building society accounts referred to at (1) above are shown on the schedule of bank and building society accounts operated which was incorporated on the report prepared on my behalf by   and dated   .

Signed   ....

Date   ....

WITNESS   (Signature ....

        (

        (Name..

        (

        (Address..

        (

        (Date..

FALSE STATEMENTS CAN RESULT IN A CRIMINAL INVESTIGATION WITH A VIEW TO PROSECUTION

TAX OFFENCES

CERTIFICATE OF FULL DISCLOSURE

Where it has been established that you have understated your income, profits or gains or failed to notify your chargeability to tax, or that your VAT returns do not accurately reflect your VAT liability, HM Revenue & Customs will normally ask you to certify that you have made a complete disclosure of all the facts about your tax affairs for the period under review.

This will give you the chance to consider the statements you have made to HM Revenue & Customs. If at some later date it is found that the statements were materially incorrect HM Revenue & Customs will take a serious view of the false completion of the certificate and any loss of tax which may have arisen as a result.

Before you complete the certificate please consider the wording most carefully. If you consider there are any facts relating to your tax affairs or any assets held that you have not given details of; then inform the Officer of Revenue & Customs of these before you sign the certificate.

False statements can result in prosecution

Issued by
HM Revenue & Customs

Do not underestimate the importance of this document – HMRC are not joking when they say that false statements can result in prosecution.

59. Interest

Whether or not a tax enquiry ends with penalties being charged, interest will be payable on any additional tax found to be due. This runs at a rate of (currently) 3% from the date the tax would have been paid if the return had been correct up to the date on which the tax is actually paid.

60. Compliance Visits

Compliance visits typically involve taxes a business is required to collect on behalf of HMRC, such as PAYE on wages, VAT, or deductions under the Construction Industry Scheme. They may also be in connection with the National Minimum Wage legislation.

If at all possible, it is wise to have a tax adviser present at such a visit, and if you have a good Fee Protection policy (see Tip 66) this should pay for the cost of this.

These compliance visits are much more focused on the processes involved in complying with the tax legislation and collecting and remitting the tax concerned, but do not dismiss them – they can be both time consuming and – if errors are found – expensive.

61. Employer Compliance Reviews

An Employer Compliance Review is one example of a compliance visit, and as well as checking that PAYE has been correctly operated (probably less significant now PAYE is dealt with online under the Real Time Information scheme) the officer from HMRC will be checking the treatment of taxable benefits and business expenses.

Without going into the technical details of each item, the following is a list of the ten most troublesome issues that can arise during an Employer Compliance Review:

- incorrect calculation of car and fuel benefit;
- loans to employees;
- staff parties;
- business lunches;
- clothing or uniforms provided to employees;
- living accommodation for employees;
- travel and subsistence expenses;
- telephones, especially mobile phones;
- working at home;
- 'self-employed' workers who should be taxed as employees.

62.   VAT Visits

As the name implies, VAT visits are visits to check that the business has been accounting for VAT correctly. The commonest mistakes are:

- partial exemption calculations;
- anything to do with land and property;
- timing of input tax claims;
- 'disaggregation' – for example, where a husband and wife run a farm in partnership, and claim the wife runs the B&B as a sole trader (thus being below the threshold for charging VAT to guests).

63. The 'Single Compliance Process'

The Single Compliance Process refers to an initiative currently being trialled by HMRC that it is claimed will speed up and simplify the process of tax investigations. It involves an early meeting at the business premises. Until they had to back down in the face of howls of protest from people like me, it also involved going straight to the taxpayer without involving the tax adviser!

Certainly the claimed target times are spectacularly shorter than the time taken at present on a tax enquiry. According to HMRC, they depend on the level of complexity of the enquiry, and are:

Level 1 – Compliance checks where there is no need for a face-to-face meeting, where for example the check would be carried out by correspondence or telephone, and with minimum inconvenience.

Level 2 – Compliance checks where a face-to-face intervention approach is required.

Level 3 – Compliance checks requiring a greater amount of time face to face because the depth and breadth of the enquiry is more involved than at level 2.

Level 4 – Compliance checks with characteristics that require an evasion approach.

The levels are purely indicative of the amount of effort perceived as necessary at the start of the check in order to address the risks. The levels are a management tool to ensure proportionality and efficiency. Levels should not be used to 'badge' risk.

All levels can apply to all taxes and types of cases and the level can change throughout the lifetime of the compliance check proportionate to the risks identified.

How long will an enquiry take under the SCP?

For trial purposes HMRC has estimated a maximum time to work each enquiry at each level as follows:

Level 1 – 1.5 days

Level 2 – 2 days

Level 3 – 4 days

Level 4 – 8 days

These timings represent the average amount of time that HMRC officers spend actually working through the enquiry. Among the improvements HMRC is trying to achieve is a reduction in the period over which these timings are spread. HMRC does not know how well these estimates reflect the time required by the business and agent but HMRC thinks that sharing their estimate of the timings should help to plan the enquiry and, HMRC hopes, bring about a reduction in the overall time taken to complete the enquiry.

It remains to be seen how effective this new process will be – I am sceptical about whether these times will ever be achieved.

Chapter 8.
How To Protect Yourself From A Tax Enquiry

64. Keep Good Records

The best defence is to have proper and carefully kept business records, and to make sure that the accounts are prepared in accordance with those records.

Now this may sound easy but in practice most of us are sometimes a bit lazy about it and it is very important to keep proper detailed records. If you have any doubts about what records you should be keeping, ask an accountant.

The first job of an inspector running an investigation is to 'break the records' – that is, to demonstrate that they cannot be relied on as a basis for the accounts. Once they have done this they have a justification for substituting their own estimates of what they think the profits should have been.

I cannot emphasise enough the importance of keeping meticulous records. All tax advisers – and tax inspectors – are well aware of a real case where HMRC were able to prove that *one* specific sale from a shop had not been recorded or declared in the accounts – the customer had become suspicious when she was asked to make out her cheque to a name different from the name of the shop, and had reported this to HMRC. This case went to court, and the court agreed that the proof of this single deliberate omission was enough to 'break the records' and allow HMRC to substitute their estimate of what the profits should have been.

65. Good Record Keeping – The Enquiry That Went Away

I was called in as a consultant by an accountant whose client – the owner of a pub – was being investigated by a particularly aggressive tax inspector. The inspector had (he claimed) evidence that income from sales of food and from barbecues was not being declared, and he was also suspicious about the number of times the 'no sale' button on the till had been pressed.

The landlord explained to me that he did not sell food, but he did allow people to bring their own and to hold barbecue parties in the pub garden – unusual, but he reckoned he made enough from the drink sales and did not want the hassle involved in doing food himself.

Fortunately, he had kept excellent records, including counting and recording the cash in the till at the end of every day. A strongly worded letter to the inspector pointing out that he had failed to 'break the records' was enough to get the case closed down.

66.   Fee Protection

Fee Protection is a form of insurance that covers you for the costs of professional advice when your tax affairs are investigated. The cost of a tax enquiry can be very high indeed. Take the so-called 'Level 3' enquiry under the Single Compliance Process described above (Tip 63). The time allocated is four days – say 30 hours. At £100 per hour four days of a tax adviser's time would cost £3,000, and very few advisers' charges are that low. At £150 per hour, you are looking at £4,500, and I have already said I think the timings under the single compliance process are much too short.

Most good accountancy firms offer some form of Fee Protection to their clients, and it is also possible to buy it for yourself through an insurance broker. Some trade or business organisations also offer some form of protection as part of their membership package.

Be careful when choosing – if your accountant offers a policy, this is likely to be the best bet. Some policies on the market offer levels of payment that are far too low, or are so hedged about with conditions that they are almost useless.

A final word about tax avoidance – most policies refuse to cover enquiries into tax avoidance schemes!

67.   Get A Good Tax Adviser

The difference between trying to deal with an enquiry yourself and having a good tax adviser on your side is huge.

A good tax adviser will do his or her best to ensure the tax enquiry is conducted fairly, that the information asked for is 'reasonably required', and that a reasonable settlement is agreed. It is important that the adviser concerned is experienced at dealing with tax enquiries, as this is a specialised skill and really only comes with experience.

Some accountants in general practice will admit that they lack the experience to deal with a serious tax enquiry, and will use the services of a specialist like me as a consultant. Some Fee Protection policies operate by providing the services of such a specialist.

68. Be Cooperative

Being cooperative is not the same as being weak and agreeing to everything the tax inspector demands. There is no point in antagonising the inspector, however, and we have seen the effect that cooperation or the lack of it can have on penalties.

There is an ancient Chinese book called 'The Art of War', by Sun Tzu, and one of my favourites among the many maxims it contains is, 'Build golden bridges for your enemy to retreat across'. I sometimes quote this to clients when explaining how I am dealing with their tax enquiry!

69. Be Realistic

If you have been over-claiming expenses or concealing income, admit it at once. There is no point in letting the inspector drag out every mistake through a long process of enquiry, and again, this sort of slow extraction will have its effect on the level of penalties that are charged.

70.   Be Punctual

By 'be punctual' I mean make sure that your accounts and returns go in on time, but I also want to emphasise the importance of letting your accountant have the necessary information for your accounts and returns as soon as possible after the end of the tax year.

Every accountant dreads the after-Christmas rush, when lots of clients finally get around to producing their business records, leaving the accountant only days to deal with them before the deadline for submitting them on 31 January. I have lost count of the number of enquiries that get started because of careless errors in tax returns being prepared at breakneck speed in the last few days of January!

71. Use The White Space

The self assessment tax return has several areas known as 'white space', provided for you to include explanations of anything unusual in the tax return. When I review a client's tax return before sending it to them for signature, I look at it from the point of view of a tax inspector and wonder if there is anything that might ring an alarm bell. If there is, I will include an explanation in the 'white space'.

Examples of this might be an unusually high figure for repairs, a significant reduction in turnover or in the 'gross profit margin' (the ratio between sales and profits), or an increase in investment income as a result of receiving money from a non-business source such as a legacy.

The white space is also useful for making any necessary disclosures (for example, about how a valuation was arrived at) to try to avoid the opportunity for HMRC to make a 'discovery' – see Chapter 3.

Company returns do not have a white space, but the same effect can be achieved with an attachment in PDF form.

72.   CG 34

CG 34 is an HMRC form on which you can ask them to agree a valuation with you before you send in your return. If the valuation (for example, of a March 1982 value) is agreed, then there will not be an enquiry into that aspect once the return is submitted.

It is important to submit a CG 34 in good time. The form itself says it should be submitted more than two months before the filing deadline for the return, but in my experience it is wise to submit it significantly earlier than that.

73. Know Your Rights

We have already looked at the rules governing when HMRC can begin a tax enquiry and what information they can ask for, and at the taxpayer's right to apply to the Tax Tribunal for a closure notice.

You should also be aware of the claims you can make if HMRC decide to go back beyond the 'normal' four-year time limit – that is, if they are assessing tax lost as a result of, at best, 'careless' behaviour on your part.

When HMRC go back to these earlier years, you are entitled to make any claims that you could have made at the time, even though the four-year time limit for such claims has expired.

The detail of this is complicated and can be highly technical, but it can be very important. In one case, a client of mine was able to claim tax relief for losses he had sustained five years previously to set against a large capital gain that was the subject in dispute with HMRC.

Chapter 9.
The Tax Tribunal

74.   What Is The Tax Tribunal?

I have referred to the Tax Tribunal several times during this book, and it is time to have a closer look at what it is and what it does.

The Tax Tribunal is independent of HMRC, and is staffed by a mixture of judges, barristers and laymen. The composition of any particular Tribunal will be chosen according to the nature of the tax case that is to be heard.

The Tribunal is the first port of call in resolving disputes between HMRC and taxpayers, and has two levels – the First-tier Tribunal and the Upper Tribunal.

75.   The First-Tier Tribunal

Most disputes are dealt with in the First-tier Tribunal, and only if one of the parties (the taxpayer or HMRC) appeals against their decision will the case be heard by the Upper Tribunal.

The disputes dealt with by the First-tier Tribunal will include:

- Appeals against penalties charged by HMRC.
- Appeals against amendments to returns or assessments made by HMRC.
- Technical disputes concerning the interpretation of tax legislation.
- Disputes over the facts in a tax enquiry – for example, is the cash found under the taxpayer's mattress undeclared business takings?
- Applications to require HMRC to close down an enquiry.
- Appeals against HMRC's requests for information on the grounds it is not 'reasonably required', or it would be 'unduly onerous' to have to produce it.

76.   The Upper Tribunal

This is part of the Courts system (Chancery, to be exact). Before the Upper Tribunal was set up, its equivalent was the High Court. As well as dealing with appeals from decisions of the First-tier Tribunal, the Upper Tribunal is likely to be the first to hear more complex and technical cases. Either HMRC or the taxpayer can ask for their case to be heard directly by the Upper Tribunal.

Hearings before the Upper Tribunal are much more formal than those before the First-tier Tribunal, and I would strongly advise having a barrister to represent you should you ever find yourself there.

77.   Further Appeals

If either side is unhappy with the decision of the Upper Tribunal, then the case can be heard by the Court of Appeal, and if still not resolved, a further appeal can be made to the Supreme Court. Some cases – particularly those involving VAT – end up at the European Court.

This process can take years – a recent Supreme Court decision (in May 2013) related to a tax avoidance scheme that started in 1998.

Generally speaking a tax investigation is not going to become the subject of a Court of Appeal or a Supreme Court hearing (though it has happened), and this is because of a very important fact about the First-tier Tribunal, discussed in Tip 78.

78. The Finding Of Facts

It is only possible to appeal against a decision of the First-tier Tribunal on a question of law, not one of fact. This may seem a pedantic distinction, but in fact it is absolutely vital to decisions about whether to go to the Tribunal or not.

In some tax investigations, the taxpayer and the tax inspector can be unable to agree on where the truth lies. Was the taxpayer's extravagant lifestyle funded by his success in backing horses (as he says) or from undeclared business takings (as HMRC say)? If it proves impossible to reach agreement then the First-tier Tribunal can be asked to decide.

My choice of betting wins as an explanation for available cash is deliberate – HMRC have a firm policy of not accepting betting stories, as their view is that if you have proof of a big win, you may well have a history of losses you are not telling them about.

This is also a pure question of fact – either the cash was won on the horses, in which case it is clearly not taxable, or it is undeclared cash takings, in which case it certainly is.

This means that whichever way the First-tier Tribunal finds, it is highly unlikely that either the taxpayer or HMRC will be able to appeal to the Upper Tribunal about it, because it is facts, not law, that are in dispute.

Many people are afraid to go to the First-tier Tribunal assuming that if they win, HMRC will use their deep pockets to appeal against the decision, whereas the taxpayer would not be able to afford the legal fees involved. In cases like the gambling winnings, however, there is little risk that there will be any appeal from the decision.

79. Use The Tribunal

Taxpayers – and tax advisers – should not be afraid to go to the First-tier Tribunal. Provided there is enough tax involved in cash terms to justify it, it is well worth considering going to the Tribunal, particularly as regards:

- appealing against penalties;
- disputes about sources of cash; and
- closure notices.

In some cases, it is not necessary to actually attend the Tribunal. Simpler cases can be dealt with 'on the papers' (see Tip 80).

80. 'On The Papers'

If the First-tier Tribunal deals with a case 'on the papers' this simply means that they consider written arguments by HMRC and by the taxpayer, and notify both of their decision by post. This is clearly cheaper and less stressful than preparing for and attending the Tribunal in person.

My last appeal against a penalty for a client was sent in with a request that it be dealt with 'on the papers'. The outcome is instructive. Before the Tribunal had had time to consider the arguments, HMRC wrote to me. They took four sides of A4 to explain that they did not consider my arguments had any merit, but that they had nevertheless cancelled the penalty!

HMRC have something of a reputation for what the legal profession describes as 'settling on the courthouse steps' – that is backing down just before the Tribunal hears the case.

81.   Going Beyond The Tribunal

As I have explained, this is very unusual for a tax enquiry, but if the dispute with HMRC involves issues of law as well as fact, and there is enough tax involved, you may consider going beyond the Tribunal.

You should not underestimate the expense of appealing to the Upper Tribunal or the courts above it – we are looking at tens of thousands of pounds, and in some cases the loser has to pay the winner's costs as well.

Sometimes, where the case is of significance to many other taxpayers, the appellant may be supported by a trade association or some similar body.

82.   You Need A Barrister

The crucial point, however, if you think your case may wind up in the higher courts, is to have a tax barrister to represent you at the First-tier Tribunal. You will certainly need a tax barrister if the case goes to higher courts, but remember that the First-tier Tribunal finds the facts in the case and only in very exceptional circumstances can these be challenged in the higher courts. Too many cases have been lost because of unhelpful findings of fact by the First-tier Tribunal, and that is why you need a barrister to make sure the right facts are found.

Chapter 10.
Examples Of Actual Tax Investigations

83.   Real Cases

The following examples of tax enquiries are based on real cases that I have been involved with. I have changed some of the details so that there is no possibility of those involved being identified.

Examining these real cases will enable you to see how the principles described elsewhere in this book work out in practice, and what to expect from a tax enquiry.

84. The Dream House

A company director came to see me – he had chosen our firm because my biography mentioned I enjoyed crime novels, and so did he.

He explained that some years ago he and his wife had bought a rundown house by a river, and had spent a great deal of money doing it up. Not long after they had finished the work, his business had got into serious financial difficulties and they ended up having to sell the house to inject money into the company to pay off creditors.

His accountants at the time had told him (wrongly) that the capital gain on the house was exempt from capital gains tax, so he and his wife had not mentioned it on their tax returns.

HMRC had opened enquiries into their returns, seeking to charge CGT on the gain on the house.

85.   The Nightmare Tax Inspector

My client had sacked his previous accountants as soon as he discovered that their advice about the house was wrong, and had tried to deal with the tax inspector himself. At the time I took over, the inspector was demanding around £100,000 in CGT on the substantial gain he claimed had been made.

The gain was all the bigger because he was refusing to allow most of the expenditure on the house on the grounds that it was 'repairs and maintenance' rather than 'improvements'.

He had been given a comprehensive list of the work done, but this did not make him change his mind. He had managed to get my client to agree that the property was not 'dilapidated' when he bought it, and seemed to think this proved that any work done involved repairs rather than improvements.

86. Reassurance

My client and his wife were both very worried about the whole matter. He had just started to get his business back on its feet, but there was no way he could afford the £100,000 CGT.

I had a look at the survey he had had done when he bought the property, and at some photographs of the finished job and the sales particulars from when he sold it, together with the invoices and the details of the sums paid into his company to satisfy creditors.

I told my client that nearly all the expenditure would qualify as improvements and that in addition, the sums he had had to pay to the creditors of his company, together with the fact that the shares in the company had become worthless, meant that there were substantial losses that could be set against the capital gain.

My client could not remember whether he and his wife had claimed these losses at the time, but I reassured him that in any event he would be able to make late claims for them because the CGT related to an out-of-date year – in these circumstances, the taxpayer can make any claims that could have been made at the time if the tax had been collected in the normal way (Tip 73).

87.   The Inspector Digs In

I wrote to the inspector making all the above points, and he simply refused to agree any of them. He still asserted that the work on the house was repairs, and he flatly denied that my client was entitled to make late claims for the losses.

To cut a very long story short, it was only after I had reluctantly made a formal complaint about the inspector's conduct and asked for the case to be reviewed by someone higher up the food chain, that we got a reply enclosing a 'technical note' that had been sent to the inspector.

This told him he should be prepared to accept a large proportion of the work on the house as 'improvements' and thus allowable for CGT purposes, and that he was technically incorrect to refuse the claims for losses.

There was also a redacted paragraph that I would love to have read, which I can only assume contained some sort of reprimand for his conduct of the enquiry.

We were invited to submit our calculation of the tax due, which turned out to be nothing once the losses and the improvements were taken into account, and this was immediately agreed by the inspector and the case was closed.

88. A Happy Ending

We then made a claim for compensation for the costs that my client had incurred as a result of my long argument with the inspector on these points, and the client received a cheque for over £6,000 from HMRC, together with an apology!

I have begun this section with a happy story, but not all tax enquiries end so well!

89. Undeclared Rent

I was approached by a client who had been letting properties for some years but had not declared the income to HMRC – and nor had he been sent any notices by them to file a self assessment return.

We immediately wrote to HMRC disclosing the fact that rental income had not been declared and saying we would let them know the amounts shortly.

We sent in accounts for the previous six years, and HMRC responded by assessing the previous four years so that interest could be charged on the tax due, but did not impose any penalties. They decided the tax due for the previous two years was too small to bother about.

This just goes to show the importance of disclosure – they presumably took the view that failing to notify them of the rental income was 'careless' and as this was an 'unprompted disclosure' and we had been cooperative, the penalty due was nil – see the table in Tip 22.

90.   The Paperless Restaurant

Not all tax enquiries end well. I was called in to advise on an enquiry into a restaurant that had dreadfully poor records. The proprietor was in the habit of noting down the day's takings in a school exercise book and then destroying the bills.

This was bad enough, but in addition, HMRC had discovered two pages of the exercise book that apparently covered the same couple of weeks, and the figures on each were different for the same days!

In other words, HMRC had comprehensively 'broken the records' so the only question was what profit figure was to be substituted for the obviously incorrect one in the accounts.

91.   Business Economics

HMRC will use the 'business economics' approach to reconstruct accounts when the records cannot be relied on. It works on the assumption that even if takings have not been declared, the taxpayer will have claimed all the expenses that he or she can.

You then look at comparable ratios between costs of food and sales in other similar restaurants, and use these to work out a probable figure for the actual takings.

The problem here is that HMRC have all the information they could wish for about the actual results of restaurants in the area, whereas the taxpayer only has such sources as trade journals to estimate the sort of returns to be expected from restaurants of the same type.

The list of comparable profit ratios prepared by the inspector was of course anonymous, so it was difficult to challenge, but we had some debate about it, followed by a rather acrimonious meeting at which HMRC gave the taxpayer an ultimatum – either he agreed to the figures they proposed (slightly revised downwards as a result of my observations), or they would go to the Tax Tribunal and ask them to confirm significantly higher figures. Faced with effectively worthless records, I had to advise the taxpayer to take the offer. The settlement included penalties of around 35% – the system for calculating penalties was different then, and under today's system the penalties (for a prompted disclosure of deliberate inaccuracy with concealment) would have been over 50%.

92.   The Golfing Builder

This was an 'Employer Compliance Review', and one of the main issues, together with some inaccuracies in calculating car benefit, was the treatment of the costs of a number of golfing days.

These had been disallowed in the accounts as 'business entertainment' but HMRC were claiming that in fact they should be taxed as benefits in kind, as the purpose of the expenditure by the company was to enable the taxpayer to enjoy himself, not to entertain clients.

The fact that the 'clients' who were invited were always the same people, and they invited the taxpayer to golfing days in return, did not help our case, and in the end we agreed a compromise with half the costs treated as benefits in kind for the taxpayer. There were no penalties, as after all, this was really a matter of opinion.

93.   The Hidden Swimming Pool

After an enquiry was started into his company's accounts, a client admitted to me that invoices apparently for a very large and expensive piece of plant installed in his factory were partly – more than 50% actually – for the installation of a swimming pool in the basement of his large house! He also told me about certain dealings involving an offshore trust that were essentially fraudulent and involved diverting money from the company to the Channel Islands.

I rang one of my contacts in what was then HMRC's Enquiry Branch, and arranged for my client to be given the then equivalent of the Contractual Disclosure Facility, having warned him that there was a very real risk of criminal prosecution.

After a great deal of expensive work reconstructing the amounts of tax that had been evaded, the case was eventually settled.

Once again, this was under the old system of penalties, and the penalty was 38% of the tax evaded. Today, it would be 50%.

94.   Repairs Or Improvements (1)

A client owned a house (not his main residence) in a seaside resort, which he used as a weekend retreat. When he bought it, he spent a considerable amount of money on improvements, including a designer kitchen to replace the old 'utility' one dating from the 1950s, and an Adam fireplace to replace the brick and electric fire from the previous owner.

When he sold the house, HMRC tried to argue that neither of these were 'improvements', and thus allowable for tax, because 'one kitchen is much like another'.

95.   Repairs Or Improvements (2)

Another client put a new kitchen into one of his letting properties. It was, I suppose, an 'improvement' in the sense that the old kitchen was rather tired and scruffy, but it involved the same basic amenities.

As you will have no doubt guessed, this time, HMRC were convinced the new kitchen was an 'improvement' and not a 'repair' that could be set against the rental income.

96.   The Cash-In-Hand Man

A client in the building trade was investigated for failing to operate PAYE properly on his men's wages. HMRC were able to produce a note in the client's handwriting (no doubt supplied by a disgruntled former employee) in which he refused to agree an increase in the hourly rate on the grounds that 'you get £10 per day in your back pocket with no questions asked'.

Needless to say, this proved expensive for the client, who had to pay the PAYE and National Insurance he should have deducted from these daily £10s he was paying all of his employees!

97.   The Equestrian Business

A wealthy client's wife and daughter ran a livery stable at their country house, and HMRC investigated the fact that for a number of years it had been making losses that were being claimed against the client's income (he was a partner in the business).

Losses in a trade can only be claimed against other income in cases where the trade is run on a commercial basis, and with a view to profit.

We had a bit of an argument but when it was pointed out that the business was changing and adapting in order to try to reduce the losses, the inspector eventually agreed the claims could continue.

Chapter 11.
Conclusions

98.   What Have We Learned?

In this book we have looked at every type of tax enquiry, from a simple 'aspect' enquiry where (for example) the inspector looks at whether all the 'repairs' claimed are in fact repairs and not capital expenditure, to the deadly serious and potentially life changing fraud investigation under the Contractual Disclosure Facility.

We have also looked at the related topic of tax avoidance, and the ways in which HMRC seek to counter it.

Remember, tax evasion is a criminal offence and involves dishonesty of some kind, whereas tax avoidance is perfectly legal. Much of HMRC's PR in the last few years has been aimed at blurring the distinction between these two entirely different activities.

It goes without saying that you should never engage in tax evasion. Leaving aside any moral aspect, dishonesty in your tax affairs lays you open to much stressful pressure from HMRC, high professional fees for negotiating a settlement of the matter, and in the worst case, prison.

Whether or not you choose to engage in tax avoidance is up to you. It is important to distinguish between tax planning and tax avoidance.

Tax planning involves making sure you pay no more tax than necessary, and that you claim all the tax reliefs available to you. It also includes specific actions designed to reduce your tax, such as investing in the Enterprise Investment Scheme, which provides a 30% tax relief on the sum invested.

Tax avoidance involves more elaborate planning designed to exploit the legislation in order to produce a reduction in tax not intended by Parliament, according to HMRC.

The difficulty lies in deciding which side of the line a tax planning idea falls!

99.   Tax Planning or Tax Avoidance?

In the last couple of years, much anti-avoidance legislation has been introduced to counter what used to be regarded as commonplace tax planning.

For example:

- It used to be standard practice for more profitable and larger partnerships (including most of the top accountants and law firms!) to include a limited company as one of the members of the partnership. This enabled them to shelter some of their profits from the high rates of personal income tax, and instead to pay corporation tax on those profits at 20%. Legislation in the 2014 Finance Act made such 'avoidance' unworkable.

- Until 2015, if you had a successful sole trader business or partnership, you could transfer this into a company and pay capital gains tax at 10% on the value of the business including goodwill. The company could then write down the goodwill (as required by accounting standards) and claim a deduction for this. This was seen as a 'perk' from incorporating the business, and most incorporations were done for valid commercial reasons, and it came as a real surprise when the pre-election 2015 Budget and Finance Act removed Entrepreneur's relief on goodwill sold to a connected company, and denied that company a deduction for its writing down of goodwill.

These are just two out of many examples of how the goalposts keep moving, and more and more tax planning is being re-characterised as tax avoidance and prevented by anti-avoidance legislation.

There are, however, two things that you should know as a result of reading this book, and if you only remember these two, it will mean the time spent reading has been well spent.

100. Avoid Avoidance 'Schemes'

There is a certain type of aggressive tax avoidance that you should never be involved with.

We looked at this in Chapter 6, but it is worth repeating – if you are offered any sort of complicated and expensive scheme that claims to avoid or delay paying tax, be very careful, and very suspicious.

It is not only that most such schemes don't work – you must also be aware of the potential costs and stress involved when HMRC investigate you – as they almost certainly will.

I have two clients who indulged in such schemes back in 2008 or 2009 (before they were clients of mine, I hasten to add), and it is only in the last couple of months that we have finally managed to reach a settlement with HMRC.

101. Don't Just Be Honest – Be Careful!

Obviously, you must not tell lies to the taxman, or submit accounts or returns you know to be incorrect, but that is not enough.

Make sure you keep proper records of your business transactions, and of your personal income, and either have your accounts and returns prepared by a reputable firm of accountants, or if you insist on doing them yourself, make sure you get things right.

If you are the subject of a tax investigation (and remember, some of them are done at random) then if you have properly kept records the tax enquiry should be short and comparatively painless. If your records consist of a bunch of invoices stuffed into a shoe box, then the whole process will take longer, cost more, and there will almost certainly be mistakes for which you will be penalised.

I hope you are never the subject of an HMRC enquiry of any sort, but if you are, I hope having read this book – and followed this advice – it will provide you with some reassurance and cause the tax man to beat a rapid retreat.